First World War
and Army of Occupation
War Diary
France, Belgium and Germany

16 DIVISION
49 Infantry Brigade
London Regiment
34th (County of London) Battalion
1 July 1918 - 21 April 1919

WO95/1979/3

The Naval & Military Press Ltd
www.nmarchive.com
Published in association with The National Archives

Published by

The Naval & Military Press Ltd

Unit 10 Ridgewood Industrial Park,

Uckfield, East Sussex,

TN22 5QE England

Tel: +44 (0) 1825 749494

www.naval-military-press.com

www.nmarchive.com

This diary has been reprinted in facsimile from the original. Any imperfections are inevitably reproduced and the quality may fall short of modern type and cartographic standards.

© Crown Copyright
Images reproduced by permission of The National Archives, London, England, 2015.

Contents

Document type	Place/Title	Date From	Date To
Heading	1979/3 34 Battalion London Regiment July 1918-April 1919		
Heading	16th Division 49th Infy Bde. 34th Bn London Regt Jly 1918-Apl 1919 From U.K.		
Heading	War Diary Of 34th Bn London Regt. (K.R.R.C.) For July 1918		
War Diary	Bourley Camp Aldershot	01/07/1918	31/07/1918
Miscellaneous	HQ 49th Inf Bde	00/09/1918	00/09/1918
Heading	War Diary Of 34th Bn London Regt (K.R.R.C) For August 1918		
War Diary	Bourley Camp	01/08/1918	01/08/1918
War Diary	Aldershot	01/08/1918	01/08/1918
War Diary	Boulogne	02/08/1918	02/08/1918
War Diary	Widehem	03/08/1918	19/08/1918
War Diary	Widehem Beugin	20/08/1918	20/08/1918
War Diary	Barlin	21/08/1918	21/08/1918
War Diary	Cambrin	22/08/1918	28/08/1918
War Diary	Cambrin Sector	29/08/1918	31/08/1918
War Diary	In The home Cambrin Sector	01/08/1918	02/09/1918
War Diary	Cambrin Sector	03/09/1918	08/09/1918
War Diary	Cambrin	09/09/1918	17/09/1918
War Diary	Cambrin Sector	18/09/1918	30/09/1918
War Diary		01/10/1918	30/10/1918
War Diary	Bruyelles	01/11/1918	05/11/1918
War Diary	Sentier	06/11/1918	07/11/1918
War Diary	Bruyelles	10/11/1918	14/11/1918
War Diary	Sentier	15/11/1918	15/11/1918
War Diary	Bersee	16/11/1918	30/11/1918
Heading	War Diary 34th Bn London Regt. (K.R.R.C) 1st/31st December 1918 Vol 6		
War Diary	Bersee	01/12/1918	31/01/1919
Heading	War Diary Of 34th Bn London Regiment (K.R.R.C) for February 1919 Vol 8		
War Diary	Bersee	01/02/1919	28/02/1919
Heading	War Diary of 34th Bn London Regt (K.R.R.C.). for March 1919 Vol 9		
War Diary	Bersee	01/03/1919	21/04/1919
Heading	War Diary Of 34th Bn. London Regt. (K.R.R.C.) For April 1919		

1079/3

3 & 4 Battalion London Regiment

July 1918 – Apl 1919.

16TH DIVISION
49TH INFY BDE

34TH BN LONDON REGT (~~RRC~~)
JLY 1918-APL 1919

From UK

Army Form C. 2118.

WAR DIARY
or
INTELLIGENCE SUMMARY.
(Erase heading not required.)

Vol 1

CONFIDENTIAL

WAR DIARY 9TH
3/4th Bn LONDON R4t (ARMY)

for July 1918

App 19

Place	Date	Hour	Summary of Events and Information	Remarks and references to Appendices

WAR DIARY
INTELLIGENCE SUMMARY

Place	Date	Hour	Summary of Events and Information	Remarks and references to Appendices
BOURLEY CAMP	1/7/18 - 7		The Battalion was formed & began training during 1st week. The K.R.R. & The T.F. & K.R.R.C. (moved to Kent) met the new Battalion. The Battalion had 3 other ranks Regt. M.O.R.F. & Col. F.R. Infrn. Col. Lawrence (Noyli) as first C.O. & Major Heathcote McClure afterwards D.S.O. as A/C. Lt. Col. T.P. Shenan of 17/K.R.R.C./B Command A.C. 4th Reserve 17/K.R.R.C. As Command B.C. 15.8.18. Lieut. General C.B. Egerton (later Sir) Command B.G. during the period we were in (under orders) joined the Battn. every [...] once we were made up to full Strength [...] a great improvement took place than in training. 40 officers + 690 other ranks eventually embarked for France.	
ALDERSHOT	31/8/18			

S.M.Wilson Lt Col
Commanding 34th Battalion
LONDON REGT. (K.R.R.C.)

LR/150

49th Inf Bde

Herewith War Diary for
month of August. Please

J M Wilson

O.C. 3/4th Bn
London Regt (R.F.)

9/18

Army Form C. 2118.

WAR DIARY
or
INTELLIGENCE SUMMARY.

(Erase heading not required.)

CONFIDENTIAL

WAR DIARY OF 34th Bn LONDON
REGT. (KRRC)

for August 1918.

Army Form C. 2118.

WAR DIARY
or
INTELLIGENCE SUMMARY
(Erase heading not required.)

CONFIDENTIAL

Place	Date	Hour	Summary of Events and Information	Remarks and references to Appendices
BOURLEY CAMP	1-8-1918	12.30 a.m.	Left ALDERSHOT en route for FRANCE.	[initials]
ALDERSHOT	—do—		Arrived BOULOGNE	
BOULOGNE	2-8-1918		Left BOULOGNE by train. Detrained at SAMER. Billeted in WIDEHEM & RETURNE. See Appendices	[initials]
WIDEHEM	3-8-18		Preliminary arrangements for training carried out	[initials]
	4-8-18		Church Parades held.	[initials]
	5-8-18		Training commenced & carried out without any special event. 2/Lt J.A. Scotland went to hospital on	[initials]
	14-8-18		taking place during this period. 8/8/18	[initials]
	15-8-18		Battalion Photograph took place at WIDEHEM. "B" "G" gained highest percentage of points	[initials]
	16-8-18		Battalion attended a lecture by Lt. Col. Campbell. D.S.O. (P.M.T.)	[initials]
	17-8-18		Training carried out. Brigade Horse Show. Battalion gained two prizes, one for the C.O's horse with 8th Chartreuse and one for the best Mule in the Brigade. Battalion gained highest percentage in Divisional Signal Course — Prize Buzzer.	[initials]
	18-8-18		Church Parade	[initials]
	19-8-18		Advance Party left to join & travel to forward area with 61 Inf. Bde. 2/Lts Th. Eyles & Lt. J. Brown were sent to hospital today. See Appendices	[initials]

WAR DIARY
INTELLIGENCE SUMMARY

Army Form C. 2118.

Place	Date	Hour	Summary of Events and Information	Remarks and references to Appendices
WIDEHEM	20/8		The Battalion left WIDEHEM & noted & proceed forward towards was made to BEUGIN.	
BEUGIN			buses. Spent the night at BEUGIN.	
BEUGIN	21/8		Proceeded from BEUGIN bus to BARLIN where the advance party brought joined the Battalion.	
BARLIN	22/8		Proceeded from BARLIN & bivouacing at SAINS en BOURSE. Route march round to CAMBRIN & relieved the 2/Bn. ROYAL SUSSEX Regt. in SUPPORT TRENCHES Brigade Sector Le CAMBRIN SECTOR	A/ladm C
CAMBRIN	23/8		The Battalion during the night began to work on the CAMBRIN DEFENCES and also carried out training with a possible later front wolf occasional shelling on the E. outskirts of CAMBRIN	
	24/8		Was ambushed the field 1 OR was killed & 6 OR wounded – all from 2b 5/71 8800 83 Pte SLATER Pm killed	
	25/8		A further casualty occurred during shelling resulting in 1 O.R. being wounded. A draft of 165 OR arrived from the European Base Regiment.	
	26/8 27/8		Nothing of importance occurred during the two days. The Batt. received orders to move forward into the night, quit protect. The A.S.A Rotterdam on 6/A/A on 26/8 m	
	28/8		We relieved the 5/Bn. SR/B in the line – right sub sector of CAMBRIN sector A - Right front C left front B & D in support	D

WAR DIARY
or
INTELLIGENCE SUMMARY.

(Erase heading not required.)

Army Form C. 2118.

Place	Date	Hour	Summary of Events and Information	Remarks and references to Appendices
CAMBRIN SECTOR	29/12 to 31/12		During this period nothing important happened. Occasional shelling with Blue & Yellow Cross gas shells. 3 O.Rs became casualties – 5 R.amal to G.H.Q. being camped through gas.	

D.H. Wallace Lt. Col.
Commanding 34th Battalion,
LONDON REGT. (K.P.R.C.)

WAR DIARY or INTELLIGENCE SUMMARY

Army Form C. 2118.

Place	Date	Hour	Summary of Events and Information	Remarks and references to Appendices
Before CAMBRIN K.9.B SECTOR	1-9-18		Nothing of importance occurred (a/c).—	
	2-9-18		Prior to gas attack which was to have taken place on 5th inst at 9 pm it was decided – one Coy to send out a party to attempt to investigate the enemy line holding TAUSON TRENCH. The patrol was organised from "B" Coy & consisted of 1 Platoon from "B" Coy under 2/Lt T.J. Forbes forming 5 reconnoitring patrols from 6 men each. At 2 am a close recce of FRANKS KEEP, AUBURN TRENCH and junction of TRAIN ALLEY and RAILWAY immediately E. of AUBURN TRENCH. The right patrol were not seen again and were totally captured. The left patrol encountered opposition at FRANKS KEEP and were driven back. The centre patrol was then reinforced. About 12 noon orders were received to return to old line. Casualties were 1 Off. + 28 ORanks missing, 2 wounded.	

WAR DIARY
or
INTELLIGENCE SUMMARY.
(Erase heading not required.)

Army Form C. 2118.

Instructions regarding War Diaries and Intelligence Summaries are contained in F. S. Regs., Part II. and the Staff Manual respectively. Title pages will be prepared in manuscript.

Place	Date	Hour	Summary of Events and Information	Remarks and references to Appendices
CAMBRIN SECTOR	3.9.18	10 p.m.	The Batt held the original line as on 1.9.18. The Post known as ARTHURS KEEP was heavily shelled	
	4.9.18	2 AM	Throughout the night the enemy shelling was below normal. A patrol of 1 OFF & 2 OR went out and reported enemy in AUBURN TRENCH. 2nd Lt E COOK M.M. + 10 OR against the Batt from Source.	
	5.9.18	12 m/n	A Patrol of 1 OFF & 4 OR under 2nd Lt CHUDLEY reconnoitred FRANKS KEEP which was unoccupied. Three other Patrols each of 4 OR left our lines at various reported FRANKS KEEP unoccupied & AUBURN TRENCH held in places by a few OR.	
		5 am	Enemy heavily shelled with gas shells – HE KINGSWAY & BURBURE ALLEY. 2 casualties 3? OR Burnt 2 KILLED & 2 Wounded	

WAR DIARY
or
INTELLIGENCE SUMMARY.
(Erase heading not required.)

Army Form C. 2118.

Place	Date	Hour	Summary of Events and Information	Remarks and references to Appendices
FOSSE TRENCH	6-9-15		Throughout the remainder of the day the enemy shelling was rather normal.	
		10 PM	The 49th J. Bd. advised the occupation of AUBURN TRENCH & MINE TRENCH by cooperation with the Royal Highlanders on our right, who were to take FOSSE TRENCH.	
			Throughout the night, a joint number (50-70 Rnds) of YK shells fell on the Rly frontage.	
		5.45 AM	A Coy under CAPT ELLSMOOR & B Coy under CAPT PALMER moved over and took FRANKS KEEP, AUBURN TRENCH & MINE TRENCH. Very little opposition was met with & no prisoners were taken. The line was consolidated during the morning and afterns communication trenches opened up to our old front from A 28 A. 6. 8. to A 22. D. 2. 6.	
		10 AM	Three daylight patrols under 2 Lts SMOOTHY, BROADHURST & BLACKBURN reported railway clear.	
		4.30 PM	A Counter bombing attack down in the front of the RH on our right & our right forward Coy (D) found n of enemy flank to our old front line about MINE TRENCH.	
		8 PM	Coy 8 PM 2 Lt R. H. had regained their post & were in touch with us. 2nd Lts A. COWAN & WM ANDREWS went to F.A. dump. Casualties 6 Wounded. 1 Farrier O.R.	

Army Form C. 2118.

WAR DIARY
or
INTELLIGENCE SUMMARY.
(Erase heading not required.)

Place	Date	Hour	Summary of Events and Information	Remarks and references to Appendices
	7.9.18		Throughout the night the enemy heavily gas shelled the Railway & AUDENCTON & FRANKS KEEP. During the evening the Battn. were relieved by the 6th Som.L.I. & moved out to VILLAGE LINE the relief was complete by 2 a.m. 8.9.18. Casualties. 2nd Lts LEWIS & MACKENZIE to F.A. sick O.K. 2 Killed 1 Wounded 1 Gassed. During the day a Daylight Patrol under 2/Lt SMOOTH went out to the Railway Embankment and to O.P. 6. Two of the patrol were wounded & 2/Lt. TODD & 2/c COOPER volunteered to bring the wounded down & under M.G. & Rifle fire led a cleaning ambulance through to where they have since been awarded the Military Medal.	
	8.9.18		The Battn. started by a support by Village Line & were relieved by the NORTHUMBERLAND FUSILIERS at 10.30 p.m. & then moved out to billets in CAMBRIN.	

WAR DIARY
or
INTELLIGENCE SUMMARY

(Erase heading not required.)

Army Form C. 2118.

Place	Date	Hour	Summary of Events and Information	Remarks and references to Appendices
CAMBRIN	9.9.18		2nd Lt. R.I. COWAN returned from F.A. to DUTY. BATTN. Remained in CAMBRIN until the evening of the 13th	
	13.9.18	10.30p	The Battn. marched up to relieve the 1/6 @ 10.m.21 also the relief AUCHY VILLAGE & Outskirts. The relief was complete by 10.30 p.m. Battn. H.Q. was in ROBERTSON'S TUNNEL.	
	14.9.18	5.30am	Other Enemy having gone (YX) relieved AUCHY VILLAGE & line of trenches W. of AUCHY. A patrol of 1 OFF & 2 OR under 2/Lt E. COOK 11/X left post at A 23 9 60, as to reconnoitre enemy	
		11 P.M.	M.G. post at A 30 a 2.8. No enemy was encountered & the post was unoccupied. Casualties 4 OR. 3a0 + 1 OR. S.W.	
	15.9.18	5.AM	The enemy shelled AUCHY VILLAGE, with H.E. T. YK." Throughout the remainder of the day situation was normal. Patrols had to be postponed owing to gas. 2nd Lt. TATE R.M. & 2nd Lt. MARSHALL O.C.B. joined the Batty. for Duty from R.I.F.	

Army Form C. 2118.

WAR DIARY
or
INTELLIGENCE SUMMARY.
(Erase heading not required.)

Instructions regarding War Diaries and Intelligence Summaries are contained in F. S. Regs., Part II. and the Staff Manual respectively. Title pages will be prepared in manuscript.

Place	Date	Hour	Summary of Events and Information	Remarks and references to Appendices
	16.9.18	5 A.M.	Heavy enemy shelling W. of AUCHY VILLAGE. throughout the remainder of the day Normal	
		11 PM	Two patrols each 1 NCO + 3 men went out to reconnoitre ground in front of own posts. They reported ground in good condition + very little wire. No enemy were encountered. Casualties 1 Off. 14 O.R. Sowerd 2nd Lt WOOD. A. Lt. Oxley Sowerd	
	17.9.18		Situation was normal throughout the day + the Bath. were relieved by the 6th Som. L.I. by 10.30 p.m. + move out into support in VILLAGE LINE. D.H.Q. at BRADDELL POINT. Casualties 1 Off. Wounded 19 O.R. Square Left RACE. T.G. Left Oxley Wounded	

Army Form C. 2118.

WAR DIARY
or
INTELLIGENCE SUMMARY.
(Erase heading not required.)

Instructions regarding War Diaries and Intelligence Summaries are contained in F. S. Regs., Part II. and the Staff Manual respectively. Title pages will be prepared in manuscript.

Place	Date	Hour	Summary of Events and Information	Remarks and references to Appendices
CAMBRIN SECTOR	18.9.18 19.9.18 20.9.18		Batt. Relieved in VILLAGE LINE CASUALTIES 19.9.18 12 O.R. wound in support	
	21.9.18	8 PM	Batt'n moved up & relieved 18 Ser. 31st AUCHY VILLAGE. Relief completed by 11 P.M. 10 O.R. wound	
	22.9.18	5 AM 10 PM	Enemy heavily shell front E of AUCHY A fighting patrol was ordered by the HQ Bde Cdr to capture the garrison of enemy post at A 24 C.05.60 The patrol under 2nd Lt BLACKBURN (4/1R OR) surrounded the post but it was not manned. Casualties 1 off. ~ 10 O.R. wound	2nd Lt RICHARDS F.R. left the Bath. wound 2nd Lt LEWIS D.W. Pyrexia " for Hospital

Army Form C. 2118.

WAR DIARY
INTELLIGENCE SUMMARY
(Erase heading not required.)

Army Form C. 2118.

Place	Date	Hour	Summary of Events and Information	Remarks and references to Appendices
	23.9.18	5 to 6 am	Enemy heavily shelled the whole of HUGHT VILLAGE with HE + OYY shells. Throughout the remainder of the day the situation was normal.	
		10 p.m.	A patrol consisting of 2/Lt SPANGER. R.E, 2/Lt E.COOK M.M + 2 O.R. Penetrated the front at H.24.c.05.60. + the roads running E.N + S. from it. enemy was encountered. Casualties 1 O.R. WOUNDED.	
	24.9.18		Throughout the day the situation was normal + the Bttn were relieved by the 6 Sth D.L. the relief being complete by 11.30 p.m. + the Bttn moved out to billets in Dunkirk	
	25.9.18 26.9.18		Bttn. Remained in billets in Dunkirk	
	27.9.18		All O.Rs Myers Batt to Janie de Mone 2 O.R. Joined	
	28.9.18 29.9.18 30.9.18		Bttn Remained in Jannes de Mone	

WAR DIARY
or
INTELLIGENCE SUMMARY

Army Form C. 2118.

Place	Date	Hour	Summary of Events and Information	Remarks and references to Appendices
			Throughout the month the following Drafts of 9 Officers & men have arrived from 16th Divisional Reception Camp:-	
			2 Sept. 166 ORs	
			4 Sept. 8 "	
			19 " 5 "	
			27 " 35 "	

R. Smith Capt
Major
Commanding 8/4th Battalion
LONDON REGT. (P.O. Ris.)

49
34 London Regt (K.R.R.C.) Army Form C 2118
Oct - 1918
Vol 4

WAR DIARY
or
INTELLIGENCE SUMMARY.
(Erase heading not required.)

Place	Date	Hour	Summary of Events and Information	Remarks and references to Appendices
	Oct 1st to 3rd		Inclusive The Batty continued training at NOEUX-LES-MINES	
	Oct 4	12 noon	The Batty moved off to ANNEQUIN FOSSE arrived at 4.00, & took up a reserve position on RAILWAY EMBANKMENT - "VILLAGE LINE".	
	Oct 5		} continued in reserve	
	" 6			
	" 7			
	Oct 8	11·00	The Batt. moved back to DROUVIN CAMP.	
	Oct 15		LT.COL E.B WILSON returned from leave to UK and resumed command of the Batty.	
	Oct 8 to 16"		Training at DROUVIN	

Army Form C. 2118.

WAR DIARY
or
INTELLIGENCE SUMMARY.
(Erase heading not required.)

Instructions regarding War Diaries and Intelligence Summaries are contained in F. S. Regs., Part II. and the Staff Manual respectively. Title pages will be prepared in manuscript.

Place	Date	Hour	Summary of Events and Information	Remarks and references to Appendices
	Oct 17	1200	The Batty marched up to ANNEQUIN FOSSE arriving at 16.00 and billeted for the night	
	Oct 18	08.30	The Batty moved on & arrived at DOURIN from 12:00 to 14:00 & they proceeded to PROVIN arriving 17:00	
	Oct 18 continued		Capt P.F. SMITH proceeded on 14 days leave to UK & 2 Lt P. GOWAN assumed duties & Adjutant.	
	Oct 19		The Batty marched across the HAUTE DEULE CANAL to PONT THIBAUT arriving at 16:00	
	Oct 20		The Batty moved off at 09.30 arriving at TEMPLEUVE at 12.30 moving off again at 14:00 marched on to COBRIEUX and billeted for the night	
	Oct 21		The Batty moved off at 13:00 & marched to SENTIER arriving at 17:00	
	Oct 22 & 24		The Batty remained at SENTIER.	
	Oct 25		Lt C.G. DIXON joined the Batty.	

WAR DIARY
or
INTELLIGENCE SUMMARY.
(Erase heading not required.)

Army Form C. 2118.

Place	Date	Hour	Summary of Events and Information	Remarks and references to Appendices
	Oct 25		The Batty marched off at 17.00 from SENTIER and arrived at TAINTIGNIES at 18.30.	
	Oct 28		Capt R.J. Rose rejoined from hospital	
	Oct 30		2. Sgt BAYLISS, 2 G.E. WEIR D.C.M. & 2 Lt E. REAH left the Batty. Wounded. 2 O.R. killed	
	Oct 28		A G.X. shell fell on one of the Batty billets during the bombardment of TAINTIGNIES & 5 O.Rs died of wounds & 10 others were injured.	
	Oct 25		D coy moved up into support at LONGUE SOULT	
	"		C " " " " " ST MAUR	
	Oct 26		A " " " " " " " LONGUE SOULT	Blue & H.E.?
	Oct 29		During the night of Oct 29/30 ST MAUR was shelled with approx 1500 Yh shells & but 100 gas casualties were sustained none of which proved fatal.	
	Oct 30		During the night Oct 30-31 D coy relieved C coy who returned to TAINTIGNIES. Leaving Oct 30 the Batty stood by in support as follows At 6 coys LONGUE SOULT, D coy in ST MAUR, C+HQ coys in TAINTIGNIES	

T.W. Wilson Lt Col
cmdg 344th London K.F.M.C.

34 Honktry R

Vol 5

WAR DIARY
or
INTELLIGENCE SUMMARY.
(Erase heading not required.)

Army Form C. 2118.

Instructions regarding War Diaries and Intelligence Summaries are contained in F. S. Regs. Part II. and the Staff Manual respectively. Title pages will be prepared in manuscript.

Place	Date	Hour	Summary of Events and Information	Remarks and references to Appendices
BRUYELLES	Nov 1		The Batt. relieved 18th Manchester in the outpost line. When BRUYELLES was held by the Batt, Lieut. SCOTT A+B Coy formed the outpost line, Bombs with HQ at CoY HQ offset V.19.D 60.85 support C Coy in reserve.	
	Nov 2nd		Quiet with slight gas shelling from the north. under the command of Capt. W.W. Palmer.	
	Nov 3rd		A number of posts was carried out by B Coy. The Western out to Coy is H.E. Smithetts. Le BRUYELLE approximately V.20.a.1.8 and V.20.b.9.2 with a view to establishing posts. it patrols immediately south of ANTOING. One patrol was employed. Three sections of C Coy the rifle men whole filed under 2nd Lt Smithetts ordered to map up the area to south of V20 Central Artillery & M.G. in the line & heavily shelled from V20 b & B machine gun and small arms of Provelle relieved at 1610 hours. At 1610 hours the artillery opened fire & machine guns gave additional support. The Huns Machine was 2nd Lieut's Lt Lewis Lt Tylor & 2nd Lt C.B. Marshall wd. wounded. At 1620 slightly followed by A/L Lt Smothey's Section. From the enters troops noted in the form of machine gun fire and gas shelling was brought to bear on our advancing troops. Enemies both

WAR DIARY
or
INTELLIGENCE SUMMARY.
(Erase heading not required.)

Army Form C. 2118.

Place	Date	Hour	Summary of Events and Information	Remarks and references to Appendices
			...stated that the enemy had no intention of allowing the capture of this area without a hard fight. 2/Lt A.Y. Smothy had wriggled to the extreme left & was still sniping at his post. 2/Lt Kempster & his Platoon reached their objective on the left but the other two Platoons were suffering from M.G. fire from established positions at approximately 1430 Kempster was sent for to return to the original line.

The casualties were - 2/Lt A.Y. Smothy died of wounds, 35 other ranks gassed and wounded; 2/Lt C.C.B. Marshall and 6 other ranks missing. 4 of the 5 missing other ranks were eventually found | |

WAR DIARY
or
INTELLIGENCE SUMMARY.

(Erase heading not required.)

Army Form C. 2118.

Place	Date	Hour	Summary of Events and Information	Remarks and references to Appendices
SENTIER	Nov 3		The Batt was relieved after dark by 5th Royal Irish Fusiliers and marched to SENTIER	
	Nov 4		Orders for a further move to BACHY were cancelled and the Battalion remained in SENTIER resting and cleaning up.	
BRUYELLES	Nov 10		As a consequence of an enemy retreat the Batt moved forward to BRUYELLES.	
	Nov 11		Following the signing of the general armistice the Batt received orders to "stand fast".	
	Nov 12-14		The Batt remained in billets at BRUYELLES and light advanced training was carried out. A thorough search of the area of the recent operation undertaken on 5th Nov was carried out. Sharps notices that the enemy defences had been very skilfully arranged in depth and that Machine Gun posts had been in most cases very well sited. I have also noted that some were still intact and that both the wire and the machine gun posts had not been touched by the artillery fire. The fact was the position impregnable on the S.E. Bozeres of Army.	

(31975) Wt W2353/P360 600,000 12/17 D.&A.L. Sch Btn Forms/C2118/15

WAR DIARY
or
INTELLIGENCE SUMMARY.
(Erase heading not required.)

Army Form C. 2118.

Place	Date	Hour	Summary of Events and Information	Remarks and references to Appendices
SENTIER	Nov 15		rest of the five missing men were found having been buried by the Germans. These bodies were recovered and buried with full military honours in BRAYELLES CEMETERY on 13th Nov.	
	Nov 16		The Batt marched to SENTIER	
BERSÉE			March continued via ORCHIES and AUCHY to BERSÉE	
	17,6,21		Reorganisation & training	
	Nov 22		2/Lt A.F. Williamson 2/Lt W.C. Parsons + 2/Lt W.C. Barrett joined the Batt. Capt R.G. Race took over command of "C" Coy vice Capt R.B. Schofield appointed Batt educational officer.	
	22 to 30th		The remainder of the month was devoted to recreational training, salvage work and the inauguration of a Batt educational scheme.	

Commanding 34th Battalion,
LONDON REGT. (K.R.R.C.)

Army Form C. 2118.

WAR DIARY
or
INTELLIGENCE SUMMARY.
(Erase heading not required.)

WAR DIARY

3/4th Bn London Regt (K.R.R.C.)

1st/31st DECEMBER 1918.

Army Form C. 2118.

WAR DIARY
or
INTELLIGENCE SUMMARY.
(Erase heading not required.)

Instructions regarding War Diaries and Intelligence Summaries are contained in F.S. Regs., Part II. and the Staff Manual respectively. Title pages will be prepared in manuscript.

Place	Date	Hour	Summary of Events and Information	Remarks and references to Appendices
BERSÉE	1.12.18		Parade service in the morning at 10.00 hours on the aerodrome. Football in the afternoon. The Bn. Rugby team lost in a pull round against the 6th Lond. R.	
"	2.12.18		A draft of 50 O.R. joined the Bn. Parades & salvage work as usual. The draft was inspected by the C.O. The first class held under the Education scheme met today. Football in the afternoon.	D.g.
"	3.12.18		Parades & salvage work & education as usual. Football in afternoon. Anti-aircraft guards were discontinued between 17.30 hrs & newly joined drafts on Education + Demonstration.	D.g.
"	4.12.18		Battalion Ceremonial Parade at 11.15 hours. Football as usual.	D.g.
"	5.12.18		Brigade Ceremonial Parade at 10.30 hours. Football as usual. The Bn. was beaten today.	P.g.
"	6.12.18		Parades, salvage work, education as usual. The Bn. Debating Society met in the Showroom at 17.30 hours. The subject for debate was "That the Scheme for Demobilization is a good one". Motion accepted by 1 vote	D.g.

Army Form C. 2118.

WAR DIARY
or
INTELLIGENCE SUMMARY.
(Erase heading not required.)

Instructions regarding War Diaries and Intelligence Summaries are contained in F. S. Regs., Part II. and the Staff Manual respectively. Title pages will be prepared in manuscript.

Place	Date	Hour	Summary of Events and Information	Remarks and references to Appendices
BERSEE	7.12.18		Parades, salvage, education & football as usual.	DG
	8.12.18		Parade service 10.00 hours. football as usual	DG
	9.12.18		Parade salvage, education & football as usual	DG
	10.12.18		-do-	DG
	11.12.18		Bn. carried out tactical exercise football as usual.	DG
	12.12.18		Parades salvage education football as usual	DG
	13.12.18		-do- (Coy route marches)	DG
	14.12.18		Bn parade in morning. football as usual	DG
	15.12.18		Parade service 10.00 hours football as usual	DG
	16.12.18		Parades, salvage, education and football as usual.	DG
	17.12.18		-do-	DG
	18.12.18		Bn. carried out tactical exercise. football as usual	DG
	19.12.18		Parades salvage, education & football. Bn was footed today	DG
	20.12.18		Bn took part in Brigade Route March. leaving at 17.45 hours by C.O. on "My Recollections of South Africa"	DG
	21.12.18		Parades salvage, education & football as usual	DG

Army Form C. 2118.

WAR DIARY
or
INTELLIGENCE SUMMARY.
(Erase heading not required.)

Instructions regarding War Diaries and Intelligence Summaries are contained in F. S. Regs., Part II. and the Staff Manual respectively. Title pages will be prepared in manuscript.

Place	Date	Hour	Summary of Events and Information	Remarks and references to Appendices
BERSÉE	22.12.18		Parade Service & football as usual.	OC
	23.12.18		Parades, salvage, education & football as usual	OC
	24.12.18		Parades, salvage & football as usual	OC
	25.12.18		Parade service at 10.00 hours. Each Coy sat down to Xmas Dinner in its own dining hall. The C.O. visited all Coys whilst at dinner. A football match between HQ. Officers & Sergeants which was attended by nearly the whole Bn. resulted for a win by the officers by 1 goal to nil. All entertainments were kept absent until 2100 hours.	OC
	26.12.18		Bn. Route March in morning. football in afternoon. Bn. Concert Party "The AUDAX" gave its first performance in the evening.	OC
	27.12.18		Parades & salvage & football as usual. Bn. Concert Party gave a performance in the evening to which the B. & C. 19th Inf. Bde / Bn. was present at the football today	OC

(49173) Wt W5358/P360 600,000 12/17 D. D. & L. Sch. 53a. Forms/C2118/15

Army Form C. 2118.

WAR DIARY
or
INTELLIGENCE SUMMARY.
(Erase heading not required.)

Place	Date	Hour	Summary of Events and Information	Remarks and references to Appendices
BEFSEF	28.12.18		Parades, salvage, education & football as usual	O/C
	29.12.18		Parade services & football as usual	O/C
	30.12.18		- do -	O/C
	31.12.18		- do -	O/C

Miller
Lt. Col.
Commanding 34th Battalion,
LONDON REGT. (K.R.R.C.)

Army Form C. 2118.

WAR DIARY
or
INTELLIGENCE SUMMARY.
(Erase heading not required.)

Instructions regarding War Diaries and Intelligence Summaries are contained in F. S. Regs., Part II. and the Staff Manual respectively. Title pages will be prepared in manuscript.

Place	Date	Hour	Summary of Events and Information	Remarks and references to Appendices
	1919			

Army Form C. 2118.

WAR DIARY
or
INTELLIGENCE SUMMARY.
(Erase heading not required.)

34 London Regt

Instructions regarding War Diaries and Intelligence Summaries are contained in F. S. Regs., Part II. and the Staff Manual respectively. Title pages will be prepared in manuscript.

Place	Date	Hour	Summary of Events and Information	Remarks and references to Appendices
BAPE	16.18		B Coy and R.H.Q informed situation. (CRonalts) March 14. (Coy Train not at Hazebrouck	
	17		B.H.Q. front the Francisks that column at the Francisks with a body of R.C.	
			arrived	
	18		the morning of the 18th of 18th aprils the sampled of Brij of R.Q.	
	20		A. O.K. left to reconnoitre	
	21		Patrol of the Coronels & discovered Arthropods	
			B. sent south 1.30 Kpm to the 5rd 16 Bn	
	21		had to form B.Q Scrim in R.R. after France 5 has 7/8 Bligh to enable	
	22		Baralm to trace — & the map of NR to dearly by their D. (municipally	
			was to love a CR of lift at 16 bligh	
			Just Ho Core & 2 CR of lift at 16 bligh	
	23		with no further casualties the battery Centrally that total the 2nd the	
			Company strongy Bathing Cornet 3 Officers 3/0 others woundead	

signed

Commanding 34th Battalion,
LONDON REGT. (K.R.R.C.)

Army Form C. 2118.

WAR DIARY
or
INTELLIGENCE SUMMARY.
(Erase heading not required.)

WAR DIARY OF

34th Bn LONDON REGIMENT (KRRC)

for

FEBRUARY 1919

Army Form C. 2118.

WAR DIARY
or
INTELLIGENCE SUMMARY.
(Erase heading not required.)

Instructions regarding War Diaries and Intelligence Summaries are contained in F.S. Regs., Part II. and the Staff Manual respectively. Title pages will be prepared in manuscript.

Place	Date	Hour	Summary of Events and Information	Remarks and references to Appendices
BERSEE	Feb 1919 1st		Battalion dance in Canteen for	
			1 Officer + 5 ORs demobilized (Capt R B Fotheringham)	AA
	2nd		HRH Prince of Wales attended Brigade Church Service in Aerodrome Theatre. Brigade afterwards marched past HRH	AA AA
	3rd		Whist Drive held in Canteen Hut. 6 SB ORs demobilised today	AA
	4th		Battalion attended a practice Brigade Ceremonial Parade preparatory to Presentation of Colours to 6 KRRC & 6 KOYLI & Slater Cover	AA
	5th		Rant performed to Battalion in Canteen Room. Defects held in School Room	AA
	6th		Presentation of Colours to 6 KRRC & 6 KOYLI & 6 SLRs and 6 Capt Gunnington Rifles on BERSEE Aerodrome. The battalion attended and Ashwell Guard	AA
	7th		Rant performed in Canteen Room. Lt Col HS Walker Langton Came + Major C B Heathorn MC assumed Command 27 R	AA
	8th		24 ORs demobilised today	AA
	9th		4 ORs demobilised today	AA

WAR DIARY
or
INTELLIGENCE SUMMARY.
(Erase heading not required.)

Army Form C. 2118.

Place	Date	Hour	Summary of Events and Information	Remarks and references to Appendices
BERGUES	February 1919 10th		6 ORs demobilised	
	11th		4 & 2 ORs demobilised	
	14th		14 ORs demobilised	
	15th		11 ORs demobilised	
	16th		17 ORs demobilised	
	17th		1 OR demobilised. Batln. found from 4 to 26 g.a. 20 I + 1 & 2 g.a.	
	19th		5 Officers (Lt H. Cundy, 4 Lt Mt Scoland, 2 Lt T. Richards 2 Lt 2 Lt H. Croiulet, 2 Lt T. Williams DCM) + 188 ORs left for Dunkirk 6/2/15 on being Regl: attached to Dunkirk Rly Command returning to return to Army of Occupation	
	20th		Batalion short amount of No. 76 as 8 ORs demob. to col	
	24/27		Start on a cheque of no-demob-list. 11 ORs demobilised 27th	
	28		remained Rule Morby at Lasso 31 ORs include Rll. col	
			Young demobilised	A/Col

Commanding 34th Battalion,
LONDON REGT. (K.R.R.C.)

WAR DIARY
INTELLIGENCE SUMMARY

Army Form C. 2118.

War Diary of
34th Bn London Regt. (KRRC).
for
March 1919.

WAR DIARY
INTELLIGENCE SUMMARY

Army Form C. 2118.

(Erase heading not required.)

Place	Date	Hour	Summary of Events and Information	Remarks and references to Appendices
BERSÉE	March 1st 1919		Summer Time came into force	K
	7th		Spent in clearing up vacated billets	K
	8th		15 O.Rs demobilised today.	K
	12th		Revd C.G. Birou left Bn for repatriation to South Africa	K
	13th		3 O.Rs were demobilised today	K
	15th		No R/6442 Sgt. C. Poze awarded Roumanian decoration "Croix de Virtute Militara"	K
	16th		30 Officers and 5 ORs were demobilised today. Capt W.W. Palmer, Lt. d'A.A Rotherstone, 2/Lt I.A. Atherton	K
	19th Feb		Spent in transferring Mobilization Stores etc to TEMPLEUVE	K
	22nd		2/Lieut E. Cook. M.M. & 2/Lieut E.J. Blackburn and 41 ORs were transferred to 1/16th Bn London Regt. (P.W.R.)	K
	25th		50 Officers & 14 ORs left Bn for demobilisation. Major C.B. Roathuyne M.C. Capt R.F. Smith. M.C. Capt K. Francis. 2/Lt P.S. Baker. 7/W.Nc. (Parsons).	K

WAR DIARY
INTELLIGENCE SUMMARY.

Army Form C. 2118.

Place	Date	Hour	Summary of Events and Information	Remarks and references to Appendices
BERGUES	March 1919 25th		Capt. T.A.E. Davey. C.F. left Bn to join the London Division Second Army.	K
	29th		Spent in clearing vacated billets.	
	30th		3 Officers 3 ORs left Bn for demobilization. (Lieut. G.E. Weir. D.C.M. Lieut. Mallard. M.M. Lieut. S. Lewis.	K

M Nolan
Lieut Col
cmdg. 34th KB London Reg/KRRC

Army Form C. 2118.

WAR DIARY
or
INTELLIGENCE SUMMARY.
(Erase heading not required.)

Place	Date	Hour	Summary of Events and Information	Remarks and references to Appendices
BERSÉE	April 1919. 8th		Football match in afternoon v 18th Scottish Rifles. Result (3-2 against).	
	9th		1 OR left Bn for demobilisation	
	10th		Football match in afternoon v Scots Cavalry. Result (2-2).	
	21st		1 Officer + 10 OR left Bn for demobilisation. (2) Lieut. Yulston.	

J M Waters
Commanding 34th Battalion
LONDON REGT. (K.R.R.C.)

Army Form C. 2118.

WAR DIARY
or
INTELLIGENCE SUMMARY
(Erase heading not required.)

War Diary of

34th Bn. London Regt. (KRRc).

for

April 1919.

www.ingramcontent.com/pod-product-compliance
Lightning Source LLC
Chambersburg PA
CBHW081458160426
43193CB00013B/2522